joy

A Highly Favoured Life Devotional

1st Edition published in 2022
2nd Edition published in 2025

ISBN:
978-1-967189-18-2 (paperback)
978-1-967189-01-4 (hardback)

Table of Contents

Dedication

To mom for showing us a life of joy during all stages
of our lives and for constantly praying for us and cheering us on.

To the ladies that have impacted us with a kind word,
a bright smile, and a display of true joy in Christ,
thank you for inspiring us to compile this devotional book.

Introduction

"Why are you always smiling?" "How can you be so joyful in this crazy world?" "How am I supposed to be happy when things are not going my way?" These are questions that unbelievers may ask us. These may even be questions we examine in our own hearts during various stages of our life.

Many search through social media for that "perfect" hairstyle to show off. Others jump into that new outing with their friends that will make a "perfect" social media post. Some scroll aimlessly through those "perfect" blogs or posts that just will not let them put down their phone. All of them are searching. Searching for that new "joy" to make them smile and feel fulfilled. Across many generations, the idea of "joy" has shifted to views of entertainment, experiences, earthly possessions, or even external beauty. While these ideas may not be "wrong" in perspective, they have stolen the real meaning of joy away from the Source of true joy.

Our desire in this devotional is to bring the focus of joy back to the One who brings us eternal joy. Psalms 16:11 says "Thou wilt shew me the path of life: in thy presence is fulness of joy; at thy right hand there are pleasures for evermore." Would life not be wonderful if we desired "fulness of joy" instead of that new outfit that we do not need? Would it not be easier for us to spend a few extra minutes with our Friend who is everlasting instead of comparing our lives to our "friends" on social media? How amazing would it be if we could truly smile through the tears of a hard trial instead of having a breakdown every time we do not get our way. Having the joy that Christ offers is not a skill we just obtain. It is an area that we should be ever-learning.

The first step to a joyful life is salvation. After that, obedience to Him and continuing in a relationship with Him are both steps to developing into a well-rounded Christian woman every day! Our vision for this devotional is for you to step back and recognize the areas in your life that may need a "joyful tune-up" and strive to let the Lord work in those areas. So grab your Bible, a pencil, and a cup of coffee (or tea for you tea lovers.) Start your 31 day journey on the "path of life" to find "fulness of joy" in "His presence."

- Callie Shiflett | Marissa Shiflett Patton

THOU WILT
SHEW ME THE
PATH OF LIFE:
IN THY PRESENCE
IS FULNESS OF JOY:
AT THY RIGHT
HAND THERE ARE
PLEASURES
FOREVERMORE.

- PS. 16:11

Joy on Purpose

By Crystal Aldridge

This is the day which the LORD hath made; we will rejoice and be glad in it.

Psalm 118:24

I love snow! It is one of the many beauties of God's creation that I have always enjoyed. Living in the Sandhills of South Carolina, we rarely get much snow. When we did, it was a big deal. Everything and everyone seemed to slow down. We would try to take it all in. Of course, we seemed to have no choice because when it came, almost everything would shut down. I remember one year in late February. We were forecasted to have a blizzard. (At least for us, it would have been a blizzard.) We were thrilled with the prospect of building a snowman, having snowball fights, and eating snow cream. My husband announced to our three children that if one snowflake fell, we would cancel homeschool and have a snow day. We went grocery shopping to buy milk and bread because that's what you do in the South. We planned fun activities believing the bad weather would keep Dad home from work. It was going to be great! While we were at church on Wednesday night, the snow began to fall. It came earlier than we expected. This could only mean even more snow to enjoy, or so we thought. The beautiful snowflakes quickly turned to rain. I told the kids as we were putting them to bed that they should get to see more snow in the morning. Throughout the night, I would get up and peek out hoping to see snow, but it continued to rain. As my husband headed to work the next morning, I dreaded the kids waking up to discover the snow never came. I was disappointed, and I knew they would be as well.

While I sat gazing out the window, the Lord reminded me I had a choice to make. With His help, I decided to stop pouting and embrace spring. We did our devotion that morning on Dealing with Disappointment. We discussed Romans 8:28 "And we know that all things work together for good to them that love God, to them who are the called according to his purpose."

What could have been a pretty depressing day turned into a great day. We put away all the snowmen and winter decor and filled the house with flowers and colorful spring decorations. Spring was on the way, and we were ready for it. With help from God's Word, we decided to have joy on purpose! A day that I hoped would be full of making fun snow-filled memories ended up being a favorite in my memory bank, and it all started with a sweet word from the Lord. "You have a choice to make."

joy

Date:

Scripture:

On My Heart:

Today's Application:

Prayers:

Blessings:

Real Joy

By Belinda Young

For the righteous LORD loveth righteousness;
his countenance doth behold the upright.

Psalm 11:7

As a young person, I watched my dad with great admiration. He lived right with all of his being and possessed an excellent spirit in all he did. He did not think highly of himself, but he thought highly of his Lord. When I would do something that disappointed him, I would be so ashamed and disappointed in myself. But when I would do right and I would see him smile upon me, happiness and contentment possessed my soul knowing I had pleased my dad.

My earthly dad taught me to love and honor my Heavenly Father -- a Father who is always right and never wrong-- a Father who gave me and anyone else who would read it, detailed instructions on how to live and be right. When I love His instructions and obey His Word, it affects my inner being, producing a joy that is beyond anything that could be produced within myself.

He is my Heavenly Father because I accepted him as my personal Savior. He is my Father because He chose me. I am His child because I accepted Him. Thus, I long to please Him and see Him smile upon me — not just "put up with me" because I am His child. There is no peace and no contentment if I do not do those things that I know would please Him. But if I do and love those things that I know please Him, there is a peace, contentment, and a joy beyond outward circumstances.

Simply put -- to have joy -- "Be Real!"

The Lord Jesus put it like this in Matthew 23:25-27:

"Woe unto you, scribes and Pharisees, hypocrites! for ye make clean the outside of the cup and of the platter, but within they are full of extortion and excess. Thou blind Pharisee, cleanse first that which is within the cup and platter, that the outside of them may be clean also. Woe unto you, scribes and Pharisees, hypocrites! for ye are like unto whited sepulchers, which indeed appear beautiful outward, but are within full of dead men's bones, and of all uncleanness."

Pure joy comes from true, REAL, right living - not a show of myself to appear righteous - but an inner peace of clean, pure, real, sweet fellowship with my Heavenly Father.

I enjoy fellowship with friends. But if I have no other friend, there is a joy in my heart, that my Heavenly Father is the best friend I could ever have. He is there any time of the day or night; any place public or private, and He lets me know that He loves me and is interested in me loving Him and shining inside and outside for Him.

Being REAL with the Lord, loving Him, and living for Him brings Joy not obtainable by any other means.

joy

Date:

Scripture:

On My Heart:

Today's Application:

Prayers:

Blessings:

Joyful Sorrow

by Victoria Kiker

Thou wilt shew me the path of life: in thy presence is fulness of joy;
at thy right hand there are pleasures for evermore.

Psalm 16:11

Elisabeth Elliott once said, "Suffering is having what you don't want and wanting what you don't have." As believers, we all have suffered to some degree or another. The question is what does joy have to do with it? How can suffering bring joy? How can grief, pain, sorrow, or hurt be joyful? Dear reader, if the statement of Elisabeth Elliott is true, then you are more than likely suffering now or one day will. It's a sad, hard truth, but suffering inevitably touches all our lives. Maybe you are suffering the loss of a loved one, a season of singleness, a prodigal child, infertility, cancer, financial ruin, or maybe something that to others may seem small. Perhaps your washing machine has completely broken down and you're drowning in two weeks' worth of dirty laundry while waiting for finances to afford a new one. How do you find joy in these situations? Can true joy even be found when your world feels so joyless?

On July 7th, 2020, the Lord in His sovereign goodness began to teach me this important lesson about joy. I had just given birth to our fourth son, Andrew. I had a difficult miscarriage before Andrew and had been so elated to find out we were expecting again. We would have our little "quartet" of men. Life would be wonderful. However, that was not God's plan. I gave birth unexpectedly on July 1st and after only six precious days with us, the Father called Andrew home. My world began to reel and what seemed like a nightmare became my reality. I had many questions as to why, but the answers never came. Deep down, I felt as though I would never know true joy again.

Through this tragedy, I have learned (and continue to learn) that suffering is a divine calling. Scripture says, "Wherefore let them that suffer according to the will of God commit the keeping of their souls to him in well doing, as unto a faithful Creator" (I Peter 4:19). Sometimes suffering is according to the will of God. "Why," you ask? I believe the answer to this is simple: my conformity to His refining plan. "That I may know him, and the power of his resurrection, and the fellowship of his sufferings, being made conformable unto his death" (Philippians 3:10). His ultimate plan for me is to be like Him. Our Father longs for us to know Him. There is sweet fellowship found only in suffering.

So, how do we find joy in times of suffering? Simply put, we must choose it! The word joy that we find in Scripture has the meaning of blithesomeness and glee; cheerful. The word picture is not that

"I HAVE LEARNED THAT SUFFERIING IS A DIVINE CALLING."

of a cheerleader; full of energy, ecstatic for life. Cheerful means moderately joyful. True joy isn't an over-the-top excitement; it is a contented spirit of true, deep happiness. Read the book of I Peter and you'll find numerous times where suffering is mentioned. Peter himself finds happiness in those believers who were suffering. Friend, the choice is yours. You can either choose to trust, obey, and find joy in the fact that God is only good; or you can choose to allow sorrow to consume and destroy you. My assignment for you: find the most contented, pleasant Christian you can. More than likely, that individual has endured some deep, dark sorrow and has chosen to trust God, allowing Him to refine and conform. On the other hand, find a "Christian" whose bitterness is evident, and you'll find a person who has indeed suffered, but refused to choose joy in pain.

My prayer for you, dear sister, is that you choose joy! Sadly, suffering is part of life in this fallen, sin-filled world. But you do not have to dwell in sorrow. Allow our good Father to bring joy. Spend time in His presence and in His precious Word; you will find joy there!

"Joy is not the absence of suffering, but the presence of God." Unknown

joy

Date: _____

Scripture: _____

On My Heart:

Today's Application:

Prayers:

Blessings:

Bringing Joy To The Father

By Kim Thompson

I have no greater joy than to hear that my children walk in truth.

III John 4

As I watched my dear son and my precious daughter-in-law pull out of our driveway after being in town less than 24 hours (#deputationlife), I tearfully thanked God for the three wonderful "bundles of joy" He gave us! I hate goodbyes, but give me those tearful partings anytime, anywhere! You want to know why I feel this way? I'll tell you why! The knowledge that my children are walking in truth makes every day, good or bad, more joyful.

As I thought of my own children, I was also reminded that there are troubled mothers "incapable" of feeling joy because of their prodigal children. My heart sincerely goes out to mothers with wayward children... I encourage you to pray, pray, pray for your loved ones!

Even though I'm now an older mother who has reared her children, in God's eyes, I'm still His little girl. Jesus Christ was a great source of joy to His Father. My heart's desire is to please the Father in the same capacity. As I meditate on my heavenly Father and how He has made me a joint heir with His Son, my heart sings, "joy floods my soul, for Jesus has saved me," and this "joy no man taketh from you." Amen!

"THE KNOWLEDGE THAT MY CHILDREN ARE WALKING IN TRUTH MAKES EVERY DAY, GOOD OR BAD, MORE JOYFUL."

joy

Date:

Scripture:

On My Heart:

Today's Application:

Prayers:

Blessings:

There Is Joy in Obedience

By Nicole Redmon

*For this is the love of God, that we keep his commandments:
and his commandments are not grievous.*

1 John 5:3

Our greatest delight will always be found in our obedience to Him!

If I asked you to define the word obedience, I'm pretty sure that "joy" would not be found in your description. You may find yourself using words like "rules to be followed," "restrictions," or "doing as you are told without question." However, joy can and should be part of the definition of obedience to the child of God. Obedience is not always easy or convenient or even popular.

But when we obey the Lord, it will bring great joy. Obeying the Lord is for our own good. Believe me when I tell you that there is "joy inside the fence!" There is protection there. A child of God should never have the attitude of, "how close to the fence can I get without crossing over?" There is no joy in hovering close to those fence posts! You will be miserable and confused living close to the boundaries that the Lord has set up for your life. Understand that obeying Him inside the fence is for your own good. When I obey the Lord, my life seems fulfilled and THAT is joyful!

Psalm 119:47 tells us, "And I will delight myself in thy commandments, which I have loved." Child of God, find joy in what He tells you to do through His Word! There are times when I have read God's Word and came across one of those "tough" verses. Yet, when I obey what He has commanded me to do, joy floods my soul! I responded in obedience to the Word of God out of my love for Him. John 14:15 reminds us, "If ye love me, keep my commandments." John 15:10-11 says, "If ye keep my commandments, ye shall abide in my love; even as I have kept my Father's commandments, and abide in his love. These things have I spoken unto you, that my joy might remain in you, and that your joy might be full." Joy and obedience are linked together in this verse! When we obey Him with joy, the blessings will pour out into our lives. As followers of Christ, our greatest delight will always be found in our obedience to His Word.

So, the next time the Lord asks you to obey Him in a specific way, please do not do it without joy. Enjoy the benefits and protection He gives through obedience. Only when we are obedient will we know the joy that comes from the Lord.

joy

Date:

Scripture:

On My Heart:

Today's Application:

Prayers:

Blessings:

Joy In Thankfulness

By Hannah Suttle

Thou wilt shew me the path of life: in thy presence is fulness of joy; at thy right hand there are pleasures for evermore.

Psalm 16:11

Joy. Have you ever met one of those people who seems to never have a bad day? They are always smiling, laughing, and talking about how wonderful life is. Have you ever looked at them and wondered how they manage to have such a perfect life? Joy is something that everyone seeks on a daily basis; I mean, who doesn't want to be happy? In all reality, these "happy all of the time" people don't have a perfect life, but have managed to find more than just an excited feeling that produces joy. They have found the source of true joy that never stops giving. Let's talk about a few of the secrets to their constant joy.

So, where does joy come from? Many times we make the mistake of thinking that joy comes from having or receiving things. While having material possessions is nice, these possessions will quickly fade away. The Bible says in 1 Timothy 6:6 that, "godliness with contentment is great gain." Hebrews 13:5 begins by saying, "Let your conversation be without covetousness; and be content with such things as ye have:..." You might be surprised how much joy you will have when you start thinking about the abundant ways in which God has blessed you. The negative in life stands out and can be overwhelming, but when we turn our eyes toward all that God has done for us, it will change our perspective!

After realizing all that God has done for you, you will find yourself more often thanking and praising the Lord for every aspect of life. When you have an attitude of gratitude and praise, you will deepen your relationship with God. Psalm 35:27-28 says, "Let them shout for joy, and be glad, that favour my righteous cause: yea, let them say continually, Let the LORD be magnified, which hath pleasure in the prosperity of his servant. And my tongue shall speak of thy righteousness and of thy praise all the day long." There is nothing that will bring one more joy in life than having a true relationship with their Savior and serving Him with their life." There is no easier way to begin deepening that relationship than realizing what God has done for you and thanking Him for it!

Challenge: Think of all of the people in your life for which you are thankful, whether it be your pastor, your spouse, or a friend. Write them a thank you note explaining why you are grateful for them. Doing this will help you realize just how very blessed you are, the words and acts of kindness will mean so much to them, and making them happy will make you happy as well!

Joy is a win-win situation!

joy

On My Heart:

Today's Application:

Prayers:

Blessings:

Joy Without Fear

By Judy Rolfe

But none of these things move me, neither count I my life dear unto myself,
so that I might finish my course with joy, and the ministry, which I have received
of the Lord Jesus, to testify the gospel of the grace of God.

Acts 20:24

Since the opposite of joy is fear, we can truly admire the Apostle Paul when we read this verse. The previous verse tells us that bonds and afflictions were abiding with him. He wanted to finish his course with joy – i.e., without fear.

The words peace, happiness, and joy are often linked together. However, joy is grander than happiness. Joy is in the heart and embraces peace. Joy is internal, sacrificial, and very consistent. Joy is selfless – you can experience joy without personal gain. Joy is not an emphasis on ourselves but on others. Hebrews 12:2 talks of the joy that Jesus had as He faced the suffering and shame of the cross.

Joy is right and moral in the eyes of God. True joy comes only through the love of Christ given to us by the Holy Spirit. Joy is purely good because it comes from God. In fact, He promises us

> "JOY BRINGS MEANING TO LIFE."

eternal joy! Joy transcends. Joy embraces peace and contentment. It runs deep and overflows. It is a practice and behavior; it is deliberate and intentional.

Joy is infused with comfort and wrapped in peace. Joy does not need a smile to exist. It undergirds our spirits and brings to life peace and contentment – even in the face of unhappiness. It is what God wants for us. In John 15:11, Jesus tells us that He gave us His Word that our joy might be full. We feel great joy when we worship. Nehemiah 8:10b says that the joy of the Lord is our strength. The devil, our enemy, is the one trying to steal our joy.

True joy is constant, limitless, and life-defining, a transformative reservoir waiting to be tapped into. It requires the utmost surrender and, like love, is a choice to be made. It is not simply a feeling that happens.

Joy can overcome anything and everything if it is allowed (James 1:2). In choosing joy, there is hope. With joy, self-esteem and self-respect are indestructible. In its truest expression, joy transforms difficult times into blessings and turns heartache into gratitude. Joy brings meaning to life.

joy

Date:

Scripture:

On My Heart:

Today's Application:

Prayers:

Blessings:

Find Joy in the Story You're Living

By Susan Hutchens

And Mary said, My soul doth magnify the Lord,
And my spirit hath rejoiced in God my Saviour.

Luke 1:46-47

Are you living the life you planned? The past year in my life brought some changes which included an international move, a change in my life roles, some delays and disappointments, and a time of forced inactivity after a minor accident. Life looks quite different now than it did just two years ago! Maybe your life story looks different right now too. Is it possible to find joy when life turns out differently than we had planned?

We have to admit that Mary, Jesus' mother, found herself living a life story she hadn't planned. She had been happily preparing for marriage and a simple life as a Jewish carpenter's wife when she learned that she would bear Israel's promised Messiah. Talk about a change of plans! Having an unexpected child at an unexpected time, facing community shaming and possible rejection by her future husband were not easy things to face, but there was no doubt that God had introduced these changes to her life.

How did Mary respond? "And Mary said, My soul doth magnify the Lord, And my spirit hath rejoiced in God my Saviour." Luke 1:46,47 Mary rejoiced! She found joy in her unexpected circumstances! How can we find joy in seasons of change?

Look for joy! We find joy in God's presence (Psalm 16:11). Stay faithful in your time with the Lord. Don't let the most needful thing slip.

Ask for joy! Ask God to allow you to have joy in these circumstances (Psalm 51:8). Ask Him for joy and gladness.

Choose joy! Choose to have joy because you love and trust God (Psalm 5:11). Decide that you will be joyful in His plan.

Express joy! Give God the glory for your joy (Psalm 32:11). Speak to others about what God is doing in your life and the joy you've found.

What are you facing that has brought change to your life? What will you do today to find joy in the story you're living?

"Sometimes you have to let go of the picture of what you thought life would be like and learn to find joy in the story you are actually living." - Rachel Marie Martin

joy

Date: _____

Scripture: _____

On My Heart:

Today's Application:

Prayers:

Blessings:

Principles of Joy

By Rachel Wyatt

Be glad in the LORD, and rejoice, ye righteous:
and shout for joy, all ye that are upright in heart.

Psalm 32:11

Joy...when you hear that word, what do you think of? How is joy different from happiness? It doesn't matter who you talk to in the world, everyone desires to be happy. And yet, are people truly happy? It seems like everyone is seeking it and they are not finding it. Perhaps they are all looking in the wrong places.

I did an online search for the differences between joy and happiness and this is what I found...

Happiness is an emotion in which one experiences feelings ranging from contentment and satisfaction to bliss and intense pleasure. Joy is a stronger, less common feeling than happiness. Witnessing or achieving selflessness to the point of personal sacrifice frequently triggers this emotion. Feeling spiritually connected to God or people.

Happiness is caused by earthly experiences, material objects. Joy is caused by Spiritual experiences, caring for others, gratitude, thankfulness. Happiness is temporary, based on outward circumstances. Joy is lasting based on inward circumstances. Happiness can be experienced from any good activity, food, or company. Joy is a byproduct of a moral lifestyle. Joy comes from serving others, sometimes through sacrifice with no possible personal gain, such as, witnessing justice for the less fortunate, or feeling close to God.

In light of the above analogy, a true Christian should not only have happiness but be continually filled with joy. Let's look at a breakdown of how we can have true joy.

Joy comes from selflessness. Philippians 2:3 says, "Let nothing be done through strife or vainglory; but in lowliness of mind let each esteem others better than themselves." If you want to have true joy, get over yourself and go do something for someone else. Stop thinking about how to make yourself happy and start thinking of how to help others. The happiest, most joyful people are people who live their entire lives focusing on the needs of others. It reminds me of the song I used to sing as a child, "Happiness came looking for me when I started to give happiness to others. Happiness came hunting me down when I started to help with all the needs around."

Joy abides in a thankful heart. Someone once said that the quickest path to joy is thankfulness. A thankful heart is a joyful heart. Did you know it is impossible to be grumbling, feeling sorry for yourself, and "down in the dumps" while praising God and thanking Him for all that Has done in your life? You just cannot do it. Praise is the vehicle on which joy enters.

Joy comes from feeling close to God. Did you know it is possible to be saved and not feel "close to God?" How can we feel close to God? Well, let me ask you, how can you feel close to your husband or your friend? By spending time with them, of course! That is the same way you can feel close to God. It amazes me the people who go day after day without really spending one-on-one time with God and then they wonder why "God seems so distant." If you want to experience true joy, spend lots and lots of time with the Giver of true joy!

Joy is a byproduct of a moral lifestyle. If you want to have a deep abiding joy in your life, you must live a moral lifestyle, not just in your outward actions but in your inward thoughts as well. What do you dwell on? What music do you listen to? What movies do you watch? Are they righteous and pure? It just may be that these things are killing your joy. You can't watch, listen to, and think about the filth of this world and expect to have the joy of the Lord in your life. Philippians 4:8 says, "Finally, brethren, whatsoever things are true, whatsoever things are honest, whatsoever things are just, whatsoever things are pure, whatsoever things are lovely, whatsoever things are of good report; if there be any virtue, and if there be any praise, think on these things." If you find yourself lacking joy, perhaps you had better purge your "watch list" (or friend list!). Clean up your thoughts and actions and watch joy creep in. Fanny Crosby once said, "Two of my secrets for staying happy and healthy are to control my tongue and to control my thoughts. I never want to say an unkind word. I never want to think an unkind thought. If you find anyone happier than I am, I want you to show him to me. My cup of happiness is full to overflowing."

Joy can be obtained by anyone. Did you notice that none of the above things were dependent on material goods or even life circumstances? It doesn't matter how rich or how poor you are or whether life has "treated you well" or "dealt you a hard hand." Joy is not dependent on any of those things! I live in Tanzania, East Africa. My church ladies and friends literally live in mud huts with no electricity, running water, or many other of the basic "necessities" of life, and yet, they are joyful ladies. They are continually laughing and praising God for His goodness on them. Why? Because applying the above principles will bring joy, no matter what your life circumstances are.

joy

Date:

Scripture:

On My Heart:

Today's Application:

Prayers:

Blessings:

The Choice Is Yours

Anonymous

But let all those that put their trust in thee rejoice: Let them ever shout for joy, because thou defendest them: let them also that love thy name be joyful in thee.

Psalm 5:11

Psalm 5:11 tells us that we can be joyful in the Lord. However, that is a choice you have to make every single day. You are the one who has complete control over that joy. As women, we can either be run by our emotions, or we can choose to bring them into subjection. Of course, it is easier to make excuses such as "they hurt my feelings" or "this didn't go my way" to justify why we cannot be happy on a particular day. But is that really the kind of woman you want to be known as? The woman who always has something to complain about? The woman who can never be happy because things just are not going her way? I certainly do not want that to be my reputation.

Just like you chose to read this devotional today, you have to choose to be joyful today. Do not believe the lies that if you finish that project, get a raise, or just get your life in order, you will finally be happy. If you are going to experience joy in this lifetime, you will have to choose it despite your circumstances. Don't wait for things to get better, simpler, or easier. Learn to be happy right now! Otherwise, you will run out of time. Let's choose joy today!

Psalm 51:10-12, "Create in me a clean heart, O God; and renew a right spirit within me. Cast me not away from thy presence; and take not thy holy spirit from me. Restore unto me the joy of thy salvation; and uphold me with thy free spirit."

"YOU ARE THE ONE WHO HAS COMPLETE CONTROL OVER THAT JOY."

joy

Date:

Scripture:

On My Heart:

Today's Application:

Prayers:

Blessings:

The Joy of Giving

By Wanda Davidson

*Every man according as he purposeth in his heart, so let him give;
not grudgingly, or of necessity: for God loveth a cheerful giver.*

II Corinthians 9:7

According to Noah Webster, "Joy is a delight of the mind; a glorious and triumphant state." In other words, an inner condition that breaks forth outwardly as jubilation or great rejoicing.

Did you feel yourself cringe or maybe hang your head as you read that definition? "That is not the 'state' I am in!" "How can I be in that 'state' with a mountain of clothes to wash, endless dirty dishes, and another diaper to change?"

Years ago, my daughter-in-law helped me with my perspective on dirty dishes with a plaque for my kitchen. "Thank you God, for dirty dishes, they have a tale to tell, while others may go hungry, we're eating very well." My friend, who did not have children until her tenth year of marriage, helped me with the diaper issue. How do we maintain this inner condition of "giving with joy" instead of being overwhelmed and discouraged?"

First, embrace the source of joy. Psalms 16:11b, "...in thy presence is fulness of joy...." Joy comes when we are secure in our faith, understand that God's love is unconditional, and get rooted in who God is! Commit to the "I wills" of joy. Habakkuk 3:18b, "...I will joy in the God of my salvation." Isaiah 61:10a, "I will greatly rejoice in the Lord, my soul shall be joyful in my God; for he hath clothed me with the garments of salvation...." Allow the Holy Spirit to grow those inward fruits --love, joy, peace--found in Galatians 5.

Secondly, realize that God created us in His image. If we strive to be in His likeness, it will change our thoughts about others, our actions toward others, and what is important in our lives. Aren't you glad that God gave? "For God so loved the world (no exceptions) that he gave his only begotten Son ..." (John 3:16a). Jesus gave His life! Hebrews 12:2b, "...who for the joy that was set before him, endured the cross...." Read Ephesians 2:4-10 for a boost of joy today!

Lastly, practice giving daily and reap joy within. II Corinthians 9:7c "...God loveth a cheerful giver." If I give my tithes and offerings with a prayer and desire in my heart for someone to be saved, I will be a cheerful giver. If I tell the little boy with a dirty nose and unkempt hair that he has a beautiful smile instead of turning away in disgust, I will be a cheerful giver. (I may have given him the only compliment he will receive today or ever!) Be a giver! Give a smile, a compliment, respect, or compassion. Look for ways to give! Luke 6:38a, "Give, and it shall be given unto you...." Jesus said in John 15:11, "These things have I spoken unto you, that my joy might remain in you, and that your joy might be full." Just be like Jesus today!

joy

On My Heart:

Today's Application:

Prayers:

Blessings:

The Joy of Service

By Ruth Weaver

These things have I spoken unto you, that my joy might remain in you, and that your joy might be full.

John 15:11

I have heard all of my life – Jesus first, Others second, Yourself last.

Many times we change it around and put ourselves first, then others, and Jesus is last. That is not how to have Joy. Joy comes when He is first, and we serve Him with all our hearts in good times and bad. I have found over my life, that when joy is gone in my life, I have neglected to read my Bible, pray and meditate on Him. Joshua 1:8 says, "This book of the law shall not depart out of thy mouth; but thou shalt meditate therein day and night, that thou mayest observe to do according to all that is written therein: for then thou shalt make thy way prosperous, and then thou shalt have good success."

When you keep Jesus first and others second you don't have time to be selfish. Many times in the ministry people get so selfish that they lose their joy. Stop wanting everything for yourself and

59

start helping others. Think of something you can do for someone this week. When you get your mind on yourself, it can cause depression and discouragement. The devil wants these in your life. You cannot serve God in the right way when you are always thinking of yourself. Others need you. Your church needs you! Pass out tracts, invite someone to church, help do a project, be available for service, be faithful in the work of the Lord. As the pastor's wife of a small church, I know the joy that is given and received when we all work together to lighten a load. Be the one that comes along and serves at your church. Your service is much needed. As a church member, you should not allow the pastor or pastor's family to do all the work. Be there to help and encourage them. That is a service you can do; and not only do you get joy in doing so, but you bring joy to others. You may say, "I can't do a lot because I have physical issues or other things." Remember everything you do to help in the ministry allows your pastor to "… give account, that they may do it with joy, and not with grief: for that is unprofitable for you." Hebrews 13:17b. The church does not belong to the Pastor. It is your place as well!

Our family sings a song called, "The Joy of Serving Jesus;" when you serve Jesus with your heart, you will definitely have true joy.

Do you have joy serving Jesus or are you selfish in serving yourself?

Do you make up excuses why you can't serve Him?

Try today to help someone. Tell someone about Jesus and how He saved you from Hell.

Desire to have joy and show others the difference Jesus has made in you!

joy

Date: _____

Scripture: _____

On My Heart:

Today's Application:

Prayers:

Blessings:

Choosing True Joy

By Kaylena Cinereski

...for the Joy of the Lord is your strength.

Nehemiah 8:10d

Many times in my life I feel so many good things! Happiness, excitement, contentment, and blessedness - but where do I begin to grasp this unwavering true joy of the Lord, that can stand firm in my life, and is my strength? I can tell myself over and over again, "Just have Joy." But that is hard to accomplish. For this life can throw so much at me! My response towards circumstances can alter like the wind! How can I consistently have that joy that will ultimately be my strength? This is a question I have asked myself many times. I have feared that I would never be able to accomplish having this joy. It never seemed to be fulfilled.

There was a time in my life when I felt defeated in this area of not having joy. I felt like it was impossible! I was really trying! Why can't I feel it? All I felt was everything opposite of joy! I came to the point of feeling hopeless, at the end of myself, where all I could do was ask God to help and show me what I needed to do! And how good He is to answer His Children. He loves His own and wants us to live in victory! God was so good to remind me that I cannot have true Joy in my own strength, and I was trying to accomplish it on my own. I would only find day-to-day temporal happiness that faded away with any displeasure, which then led to discouragement. I was trying so hard to have that joy, but relying on ME to get it! If I would only just rely on Him, and His strength to give me this joy, then I would truly be joy-filled! Romans 15:13, "Now the God of hope fill you with all Joy and peace in believing, that ye may abound in hope, through the power of the Holy Ghost."

It can be so easy to get discouraged, depressed, hurt, offended and the list goes on. I realize now, only by His grace, that it is necessary I do everything in God's strength! I finally understood, having a walk with God is essential in this Christian life! I cannot have joy without Him; therefore I cannot accomplish having Joy, without having a relationship and daily walk with Him. Only then, will the work of having the Joy of the Lord come. James 4:8a- "Draw nigh to God, and he will draw nigh to you..." And how true His word is! The more I walk with Him, seek Him, talk to Him, the more He shows Himself to me, and the more joy I find in Him with which I am filled! A true joy that lasts! For He is my joy and STRENGTH! We have a choice, to choose Joy or not. But will only ever fulfill feeling it through the Lord Jesus Christ!

"But let all those that put their trust in thee rejoice: let them ever shout for joy, because thou defendest them: let them also that love thy name be joyful in thee." Psalms 5:11

joy

Date:

Scripture:

On My Heart:

Today's Application:

Prayers:

Blessings:

Joy In Serving Jesus

By Angie Marco

Delight thyself also in the LORD;
and he shall give thee the desires of thine heart.

Psalm 37:4

When I start thinking of all those things that I cannot control, fear of the unknown and worry kick in. I am not sure if you are like me, but when this happens, all of the "what if" scenarios begin to flood my mind. Many times these thoughts try to take control of my peace and joy. If I allow it, it will take control of my spirit. "For God hath not given us the spirit of fear..." (2 Timothy 1:7) The devil knows that our joy is valuable. He will do everything in his power to take it from us!

Serving in the Philippines has increased my faith in God tremendously. Our family came here with very little support. During our first years on the field, we learned to go without some of the things we now consider luxuries. Things we sometimes take for granted like air conditioning, hot water, washer, dryer, and a vehicle. There were many times when I just wanted to cry and complain. My biggest question was, "Are we going to make it this week?" I was letting fear of the unknown take over my joy and fill me with worry. I had to learn to trust that God would provide! Through the years, I have seen God provide for our family in the most amazing ways. The joy that comes from knowing that "God did that for me" is incomparable.

I would often compare myself to other missionary wives who could afford to have the beautiful house, the washer, the dryer, the personal vehicle, and their thriving ministry. I felt I could not be the perfect missionary wife, mother, housekeeper, and ministry worker. I really had to stop myself! Constantly thinking and dwelling on my fears, worries, and needs was making me forget what we were here for in the first place. "...to bind up the brokenhearted, to proclaim liberty to the captives, and the opening of the prison to them that are bound;..." (Isaiah 61:1)

There was so much more that I was missing. I started to look at the people that started attending our church services and their needs. The children who would come to our gate. I started falling in love with every single one of them! "Mine eye affecteth mine heart..." (Lamentations 3:51) Going out soul winning and visiting opened my eyes to a much deeper need. It changed me! I have learned that when you start thinking of others and their needs, your own needs become small and insignificant. Being someone else's answer to prayer brings a special kind of joy. Serving the people around me made me realize how blessed we truly are.

I decided I would not let my circumstances steal my joy. "... glorify God in your body, and in your spirit, which are God's." (1 Corinthians 6:20) The devil will lie to you and make you believe that your joy is not worth anything. Joy is something we have to guard and protect; hold fast to it. "...hold fast the confidence and the rejoicing of the hope firm unto the end." (Hebrews 3:6)

"MINE EYE AFFECTETH MINE HEART..."

- LAM. 3:51

Our family went through some hard times, but I didn't want to be the reason why we could not make it on the mission field. I did not want to discourage my husband because of my lack of faith. I wanted to be his biggest cheerleader! I knew I had to start talking to God more than ever. "Casting all your care upon him; for he careth for you." (1 Peter 5:7) I started telling the Lord what was on my heart. "Be careful for nothing; but in every thing by prayer and supplication with Thanksgiving let your requests be made known unto God." (Philippians 4:6) That is when He became so much more to me. He is my joy! "But the fruit of the Spirit is love, joy, peace, longsuffering, gentleness, goodness, faith, meekness, temperance..." (Galatians 5:22-23) When we have Him, we have it all. He is enough! Difficult circumstances in life help grow our love, joy, peace, faith, meekness, and temperance.

My prayer was that the Lord would help me to be what my family needed me to be and that we could be a blessing to the people around us. "For God is not unrighteous to forget your work and labour of love..." (Hebrews 6:10) After nine years on the mission field, God has provided the finances for us to be able to live in a house with air conditioning. I feel spoiled to be able to have a washer, a dryer, our own vehicle, and even hot showers now! I know that to many people, these things are not a big deal. To me, these things are hugs from God. These are blessings! "Delight thyself also in the LORD; and he shall give thee the desires of thine heart." (Psalm 37:4) It has been amazing to see God's hand in our life and ministry. There is joy in serving Jesus. It is not just a cliché. It is sad that too many people waste their time looking for joy in empty places.

joy

Date:

Scripture:

On My Heart:

Today's Application:

Prayers:

Blessings:

Joy in Life's Little Moments

By Grace Shiflett

I will greatly rejoice in the LORD, my soul shall be joyful in my God;

Isaiah 61:10a

So many times, in the hustle and bustle of life, we do not take the time to recognize that every little moment we are given is an opportunity to live in the joy of the Lord. As a born-again child of God, we have so much in which to rejoice. Take time to slow down and enjoy what may seem like little unimportant moments. To live in a continual state of joyfulness, we may have to lay aside some distractions that have possibly become weights in our life (Hebrews 12:1). Put away your distractions and give space for living joyfully in every moment.

I know personally I struggle with a scattered mind with everything coming at us on a daily basis. If we are not careful, we will set a pattern of living like a robot. With so much happening in our crazy schedules, we fail to look around and take it all in with joy. Every moment we have is a gift. That thought alone should motivate us with a desire to not take for granted all the joyful moments. If I am not careful, I will get so busy with my everyday life that at the end of the day, I will look over my day and realize that not even one time did I live in the fullness of joy. The Lord wants His children to experience joy! If we choose joy, we can successfully do both our daily responsibilities and keep a joyful heart.

Do you ever wonder why we grow weak in our faith? Maybe we have forgotten the joy of the Lord is our strength (Nehemiah 8:10). With each new day that you are given, try to get in the habit of choosing to live in joy through Christ. The definition of joy is "a feeling of great pleasure and happiness." Life is too short not to choose joy.

Ask God daily to renew your heart and mind in this area. We can all agree that a joyful life is the desire we all have. That life will only start when we learn to live in joy in every little moment we have been given.

joy

Date:

Scripture:

On My Heart:

Today's Application:

Prayers:

Blessings:

Finding Joy
in Your Season

By Kelly Gray

*Not that I speak in respect of want: for I have learned, in whatsoever state
I am, therewith to be content. I know both how to be abased, and I know
how to abound: every where and in all things I am instructed
both to be full and to be hungry, both to abound and to suffer need.
I can do all things through Christ which strengtheneth me.*

Philippians 4:11

As a little girl, I remember being asked, "What do you want to be when you grow up?" I answered, "A missionary, nurse, and a pastor's wife." A few years have passed since that question was first asked - actually, a little over fifty years. Little did I know that in some form or another, God would allow me to fulfill the dreams in my heart. My husband and I worked with teenagers for over twenty years, and that is definitely a mission field! God also gave us a special needs little boy four years into our marriage, RG Gray. He is now thirty, and at the writing of this devotion, he has had twenty-seven different types of surgeries. Then, nearly thirteen years ago, my husband became pastor of the church we both grew up in. What a season we are in now!

To say all those fulfilled dreams have been easy, and that we have always walked through with grace would be untrue. Working with teenagers is rough and being a nurse to our son RG has had its sorrows and joys - but I would not trade him for the world.

You learn quickly that you have to be happy in "whatsoever state" God has placed you. So many times, we are looking for some big, exciting thing to happen in our lives. We need to just be content and find joy in the season where God has placed us. A newly married couple needs to be content at enjoying each other together before starting a family and getting very busy with the cares of work and taking care of a home. The other day, I was talking to a young mom that runs her kids back and forth to school. I looked at her and said, "Enjoy these days, because I miss them!" Then grandkids come along, spending the night, having activities at school, candy selling.

But maybe that was not God's plan for your life. Maybe He decided you needed to be single. You can spend so much more time with Him than the rest of us ever could. You can spend your life helping and encouraging others. There may come a day when your body does not allow you to get out and do the things you once did. Look at this as a season in which you can spend more time with God in prayer for the needs of others. I love when I get a text message or hug from an older church member, and they ask, "What can I pray about for you?"

I've been asking myself the question lately, "Am I enjoying the season God has me in?" Enjoy your season right now - it all changes so fast! We all have our favorite season. I was born in Hawaii, and

"WE NEED TO
JUST BE
CONTENT AND
FIND JOY
IN THE SEASON
WHERE
GOD HAS
PLACED US."

I've always enjoyed spring the most. It reminds me more of Hawaii than any other time of the year in Texas. Some seasons we enjoy better than others and cannot wait for them to come - but enjoy the season you are in - squeeze every moment out of it. What is God trying to teach you? Who can you help through your tragedy? Does God want you to spend more time with Him?

The older I get, the more I realize that God just wants the best in my life. He strengthens me and lets me go through what I feel are trials and fires to purify me and have me come out on the other side more precious than gold. Look at the season God has put you in as a learning time and embrace it!

joy

Date: _____

Scripture: _____

On My Heart:

Today's Application:

Prayers:

Blessings:

Formula for Joy

By Larissa Bell

Thou wilt show me the path of life: in thy presence is fulness of joy;
at thy right hand there are pleasures for evermore.

Psalm 16:11

Since my childhood, I have heard the formula for joy is to follow the acronym: Jesus Others You. The Bible supports this teaching as we find many examples and commands all throughout the Scriptures to love and esteem the Lord and others—even our enemies—higher than ourselves (Deut. 6:5, Matt. 5:44, 22:37-40). Science also supports the fact that helping others and having a sense of purpose, like one does when serving in a ministry, results in better resilience and joy in times of stress and suffering.

However, Christians like me, actively serving others may come easily, but it doesn't always bring joy. Remember Martha in Luke 10:40? She was cumbered about with serving Jesus and the other guests at her house. Cumbered does not sound joyful, does it? Sometimes, serving others empties our love tank when we feel no one reciprocates or we compare what we are doing with what others are not doing.

Comparison is the thief of joy!

Comparison on a horizontal plane is the joy killer. Comparison on a vertical plane is actually an important component to finding joy. I thought of another acronym to say when I'm struggling with loving unconditionally and serving the Lord with gladness (Ps 100:2).

Jesus, Only You

When I take my unthankful, unloving, and unjoyful thoughts into captivity and focus instead on all that Jesus has done for me, I find joy (2 Cor. 10:5, Is. 26:3). We can encourage ourselves in the Lord as David, the psalmist, did and serve others - not for them but as if we were serving Jesus Himself (I Samuel 30:6, Colossians 3:23). Getting in the Bible to read more about God's attributes, abiding in His presence, and serving Him and not others will help us find "fulness of joy" and "pleasures for evermore."

Challenge: What areas of service are feeling a little dry or unjoyful in your life? Whether it's your service in a ministry at church, as a wife or mother, or in your workplace, make a list of five things Jesus has done for you in the last month - doesn't matter how small or big. I know it can be hard if your spirit is dry, but ask God to open your eyes. He does so many things for you daily, but are you failing to notice just like the people you are serving? Then list five attributes of God that you can dwell on when you start to feel unjoyful the next time!

joy

Date:

Scripture:

On My Heart:

Today's Application:

Prayers:

Blessings:

What Joy?

By Beverley Wells

...for this day is holy unto our Lord: neither be ye sorry;
for the joy of the LORD is your strength.

Nehemiah 8:10b

When I was asked to share in this devotion, I began to examine my own self and question, "What joy?"

To get past my own definition of joy, I turned to the dictionary; joy - a feeling of great pleasure and happiness. Yet, is that joy really what we are looking for in our Christian life?

Joy, I am sure, comes in many different packages, looking different to all kinds of individuals. Joy to this lost, unknowing, and dying world may look like a trip to the amusement park or even a psychotic high that comes from an empty bottle of drink or drugs of some sort. Could it be an elaborate vacation where one spends money that one doesn't have on unending entertainment that leaves them exhausted? Could it be found in unhealthy relationships that are so temporal? Is that joy? I would that your joy, as well as mine, come from that which is eternal.

The biblical definition of joy extends further than just a feeling of good pleasure and happiness. Biblical joy is dependent on Who Jesus is rather than on who we are or what is happening around us. This joy comes from the Holy Spirit; abiding in God's presence and hope found in His Word.

Since the biblical definition clearly describes what and where joy comes from, we can be confident in the eternal aspect of where we can obtain joy. Joy will only come from a life that is consecrated unto God and holiness. So, we must, with great vigor, press toward a relationship with Christ in prayer, in His Word, and service. Let nothing waver!

Of course, that does not make us exempt from life's struggles, but it most definitely gives us a rock to stand on. So, when life tries to rob you of joy by the jobs on you, the judgments of you, others who may be jealous of you - remember Nehemiah 8:10. The "joy of the Lord" is your strength, and you must abide in the Rock!

To all the mothers that are struggling; the struggle is real. I know, being a mother of five myself. You may be struggling to keep your head above water, let alone in the Word. I implore you to press on, raise, and train your children with joy in your heart. Make big of God; ever pointing, not pushing them, to Christ. In due time, joy will flourish like never before. Coming from a mother's heart, the Scripture could not be more true. III John 1:4 says, "I have no greater joy than to hear that my children walk in truth."

"O COME, LET US SING UNTO THE LORD: LET US MAKE A JOYFUL NOISE TO THE ROCK OF OUR SALVATION."

- PS. 95:1

When I look at each of my children and their families serving God in their own lives, I can truly say, "What joy!" I have that which is unspeakable, beyond my wildest dreams, and yes, eternal! They now serve a personal God, not their father's nor mine. He is their Savior and Lord. Praise the Lord!

Lastly, as you commit your life to Christ in every area of salvation, sanctification, and service, when others see you, may they say, "What joy!"

Joy is among the most unmistakable marks of a faithful heart! Philemon 1:7, John 16:22, Hebrews 12:2, Psalm 16:11, Galatians 5:22-23, Psalm 95:1-2, Deuteronomy 28:47-48

joy

Date:

Scripture:

On My Heart:

Today's Application:

Prayers:

Blessings:

Helpers For Our Joy

By Rikki Beth Poindexter

But let the righteous be glad; let them rejoice before God:
yea, let them exceedingly rejoice.

Psalm 68:3

"When I'm wanting more joy, what I'm really wanting is more Jesus. Joy is simply the signpost that points us to Jesus." Unknown

Those that belong to the Lord should have joy! Happiness is a result of our happenings or circumstances. Joy (gladness of heart), can and should remain, regardless of our happenings. Just look at the Apostle Paul's happenings: beaten, shipwrecked, imprisoned, yet he wrote the most about joy. In the book of Philippians alone, the word "joy" or "rejoice" is used 18 times in 4 chapters. "Rejoice IN the LORD." Find your joy in Him. It is a decision, our decision. I want to share with you some "helpers for our joy."

First, have faith in the LORD: trust Him. As a believer, if we can trust Him to save our soul, we should be able to trust Him for the rest of our life. Doubting Him does not help our joy. Psalm 5:11 says, "But let all those that put their trust in thee rejoice: let them ever shout for joy, because thou defendest them: let them also that love thy name be joyful in thee."

Second, focus on the Lord: spend time with Him, in prayer and His Word. We spend time with the ones and things we love. Neglecting these wonderful intimate times with our Saviour will not help our joy. Psalm 16:11, says, "Thou wilt shew me the path of life: in thy presence is fulness of joy; at thy right hand there are pleasures for evermore."

Thirdly, follow the Lord: be obedient to what He has asked. Disobedience robs us of joy. John 15:11 says, "These things have I spoken unto you, that my joy might remain in you, and that your joy might be full."

Lastly, allow Him to fulfill you: be content with what He has given you. Do not find yourself coveting others: their appearances, possessions, life, etc. Be thankful for what you have. Joy is the best makeup. Someone once said, "It is not joy that makes us grateful. It is gratitude that makes us joyful." Philippines 4:4 says, "Rejoice in the Lord alway: and again I say, Rejoice." The cause for joy is knowing, trusting and loving the Lord. Be obedient to Him, and be content with what He has given you. If you do not have joy, ask yourself these questions: Do you know the Lord? Are you doubting Him? Do you love Him? Are you obedient to the Scriptures? Are you thankful? When I feel my joy (gladness of heart) waning, at least one of these helpers is being neglected.

Go through the Word of God, and as you read it highlight or mark with a specific color the words joy or rejoice.

joy

Date:

Scripture:

On My Heart:

Today's Application:

Prayers:

Blessings:

Fulness of Joy

By Renee Patton

*Thou wilt shew me the path of life, in thy presence is fulness of joy,
and at thy right hand there are pleasures forevermore.*

Psalm 16:11

Psalm 16 is a beloved chapter to me personally for many reasons
and I count verse 11 as my life verse. While in Bible College, this
chapter hugged my heart while at a crossroads. My husband and
I were seeking God's direction for ministry. We knew He would
direct us as verse 11 begins, "Thou wilt shew me the path of life...."
God promised to show us the path, and He did! We served eight
wonderful years in a church, then my husband felt God's nudge to
move on. Thus, we did and this is where I truly had to learn where
to find my joy!

I love to teach, serve, and do abundantly at church! I always
find joy in giving and doing for others. However, this is not where
true joy comes from. After two short, yet long months at our new
church, it was evident we needed to again move on. Nine months
later, we did just that although that nine-month period yielded

many lessons for both of us. For me, I was slowly losing my joy. It became increasingly difficult to shoulder my responsibilities and truly smile. I decided I needed to seek the Lord fervently through more prayer and Bible time. This is where I rediscovered, "...in thy presence is fulness of joy; at thy right hand there are pleasures for evermore" (Psalm 16:11b). I felt alone, discouraged, and disappointed; however, for my family and my sake, I had to find my joy again. This is where I began journaling. I would write my passages, read a verse in which God showed me something new, and talk to God through words. I am a venter! So, writing was my means of venting to God.

This created a new, revived aspect of my walk with God. I was able to get once again close to God and renew my joy! Joy in spite of circumstances, people, things, or worry can be found. God promises to never leave us. His goodness will always bring "fulness of joy!"

Where do you find your "fulness of joy?"

"GOD PROMISED TO SHOW US THE PATH.
AND HE DID!"

joy

Date:

Scripture:

On My Heart:

Today's Application:

Prayers:

Blessings:

Find Joy in the Journey

By Hannah Kasprzyk

...so that I might finish my course with joy, and the ministry,
which I have received of the Lord Jesus...

Acts 20:24b

Life is like a journey, and God holds the road map. He has specially planned a route for your life. Sometimes along the way, your path grows longer than you anticipated, and you grow impatient to reach your destination. In your human reasoning, you look at the lives of those around you and expect the timing of your life to be just like theirs. You forget to trust God's beautiful, individualized master plan (I Corinthians 2:9). If you aren't careful, you can spend so much of your life longing for the next step of your life that you forget to have joy in the journey. Joy is a daily, deliberate choice. Webster's 1828 Dictionary defines joy as "passion or emotion excited by the acquisition or expectation of good." Joy comes from the inside and brings true, lasting contentment to one's heart. What are some things that can help you find joy no matter where you are in your journey?

First, find joy in God. Spending time in His presence reveling in who He is and how good He has already been to you brings joy (Psalm 16:11, 35:9, 43:4). Have you stopped to thank Him for what He has already done in your life? Start a "blessings journal" to remind yourself of just how amazing your God is (Psalm 103). Secondly, find joy in others. Invest yourself into what you have now instead of wasting all your energy longing for what you don't have. In God's perfect plan, He has you where you are for a reason. Who has He placed in your path for you to make a difference? There are golden opportunities in front of you today; don't waste them. Challenge yourself to pray for someone else and their struggles. There is nothing more encouraging than to see God answer prayers and know you had a part in those victories. Thirdly, find joy within yourself. Joy does not come from your outward circumstances, but from inwardly accepting and being content with where God has you. What lessons is God trying to teach you today that will make His destination for you that much sweeter? Find verses that minister to your spirit and display them in places where you can meditate on them. Surrender your will to God's plan and God's timing (Proverbs 3:5-6 and Psalm 37:4-5, 23).

Choosing joy is something you will have to do every day. Are you going to have excitement and expectation in the path God has you on? Or are you going to be that petulant child in the back seat whining, "Are we there yet?" Determine to find joy in your life's journey.

joy

Date: _____

Scripture: _____

On My Heart:

Today's Application:

Prayers:

Blessings:

The Joy of the Lord is Your Strength

By Kathy Lane

---

*"Looking unto Jesus the author and finisher of our faith: who for the joy
that was set before Him endured the cross, despising the shame,
and is set down at the right hand of the throne of God."*

Hebrews 12:2

When I think of joy, I naturally think about feelings of blessedness or a position of contentment. Verses that come to mind would be Luke 2:10 "...good tidings of great joy..." or I John 1:4 "...that your joy may be full..." - which describe our normal perceptions of joy. There is nothing necessarily wrong with that concept of joy, but the true characteristics of joy are so much deeper than just the outward portrayal. Let us look at the Greek definition of the word joy. According to Strong's Concordance, joy (original "chara") is defined as: "cheerfulness, i.e. calm delight; gladness." This definition certainly seems to be applicable with our definition of joy in the previous verses; but what happens when you come to Hebrews 12:2? "Looking unto Jesus the author and finisher of our faith: who for the joy that was set before Him endured the cross, despising the shame, and is set down at the right hand of the throne of God." How did our irreproachable Saviour have joy while blamelessly suffering and dying on the cruel cross of Calvary to redeem such a wretched human race? Or what about James 1:2, "My brethren, count it all joy when ye fall into divers temptations"? How are those references to joy the same? And how exactly am I to have "joy" during storms? I am not sure about you, but for me, when the Lord sees fit to put me through a trial or storm, the last thing on my mind is a "calm delight"! Rather, my natural response is quite the opposite. I am either ready for warfare or trying to fight back the tears. For clarification, let us look at I Peter 4:12-13, "Beloved, think it not strange concerning the fiery trial which is to try you...but rejoice, inasmuch as ye are partakers of Christ's suffering; that, when his glory shall be revealed, ye may be glad also with exceeding joy." Verse 19 brings more clarity to the previous verses- "Wherefore let them that suffer according to the will of God commit the keeping of their souls to him in well doing, as unto a faithful Creator." That is it! Joy is not just an emotional feeling or perception to which we often attribute it; but rather, joy is a conscious understanding that regardless of the circumstances, we know we are in the center of His will. That is how Christ had joy while suffering on the cross - because He was doing the will of His Father! So, the trials grow our faith, which in turn causes us to trust Him more; and the more we trust Him, the closer we draw

"JOY IS A CONSCIOUS
UNDERSTANDING THAT
REGARDLESS OF THE
CIRCUMSTANCES,
WE KNOW WE ARE
IN THE CENTER
OF HIS WILL."

to Him. This then brings to light that God is our true Source of joy (our calm delight), and our circumstances are not. My Pastor often reminds us: "Peace is not the absence of conflict, but the presence of Christ." You may be asking, "How can I have joy with my past hardships?" Maybe that is the wrong question to ask. Instead, maybe we should be asking ourselves, "Did the past hardships or storms draw me closer to Christ?" Whether God authored or allowed the trial - if through it, I was able to draw closer to Him - I can have a calm delight knowing it is always His will for me to cultivate a closer walk with Him.

Are you lacking true Biblical joy in your life? If so, the first question you should ask yourself is: "Am I in the center of my Father's will?" As Dwight L. Moody stated, "The Lord gives His people perpetual joy when they walk in obedience to Him." Are you in full obedience to your Father's leading? Do you have the joy of the Lord in your daily walk with Him? In seasons of weariness, let us be reminded of Christ in Hebrews 12:2 and be strengthened knowing that He is our El Roi, the mighty God Who sees me.

joy

Date: _____

Scripture: _____

On My Heart:

Today's Application:

Prayers:

Blessings:

Joy in Countenance

By Callie Shiflett

Therefore did my heart rejoice, and my tongue was glad; moreover also my flesh shall rest in hope: Thou hast made known to me the ways of life; thou shalt make me full of joy with thy countenance.

Acts 2:26,28

If someone mentions the phrase "a joyful person," who immediately comes to your mind? The personable cashier at the grocery store yesterday? Your seemingly always smiling pastor's wife? Your best friend who can always make you laugh out loud?

Without having to rack your brain, someone specific automatically popped into your mind. Take a closer look at that kind of joyful person. Is she known for smiling because she is making fun of others or putting them down? Is she happy because the ladies at church complimented her costly new shoes? The answer is no, probably not.

The person you are thinking of is likely joyful because she has a great walk with the Lord and is content through Him. Only Christ can give us that authentic joy that sets us apart from simply being

> "CHRIST CAN GIVE US THAT AUTHENTIC JOY..."

a "smiley" person. When we have joy in His countenance, we cannot help but show it in our countenance! In the verses above, the heart is "rejoicing." The tongue is "glad." (For we ladies who love to talk and often catch ourselves discussing the negative, a glad tongue would be a miracle in and of itself.)

I mean, how happy would we be if we just simply "rested in hope"? Christ's countenance not only brings us joy, but it can also fill us with joy if we let it!

Through Him, we can experience the kind of joy that will show outwardly and inwardly - not just when things go our way. It is only then that we can be that joyful person; The person who can sharpen and encourage the countenance of peers! (Proverbs 27:17)

Examine your heart. What if your friends and family were to read this? Would you be that joyful person that pops into their mind? How can you sharpen the countenance of a friend today? Write a small list of things your heart can rejoice about. Maybe share some blessings with a friend. Warning: You will not be able to talk about all of your many blessings with a sad countenance!

joy

Date:

Scripture:

On My Heart:

Today's Application:

Prayers:

Blessings:

Joy in His Presence

By Ashley Thompson

Thou wilt shew me the path of life: in thy presence is fulness of joy;
at thy right hand there are pleasures for evermore.

Psalms 16:11

As Christians, we should be the most joyful people because we have salvation through Christ! It doesn't matter what background you come from or how old you were when you got saved; the minute you accepted Christ as your Savior, you were reconciled to Him and had "...joy in God through our Lord Jesus Christ..." (Romans 5:11b).

As a new Christian, it's hard to hold back the excitement and joy you feel! You want the whole world to know how God has saved you so they too can feel the peace and joy He gives. But, as time goes on, we can get easily caught up in the busyness of life, or even get frustrated with the mundane, and we "lose" our joy. I'm not just talking about the unhappy feeling you get when you order a raspberry-filled donut at Dunkin' and find out that the person in front of you got the last one ... Ugh! While that could be momentarily earth-shattering, you'll soon be distracted by another donut, coffee, or something else, causing that momentary unhappiness to fade. The loss of joy I'm speaking of goes a little deeper than that.

As we get caught up in the day-to-day, it's easy to get careless in our walk with God. Maybe we're still doing our daily devotions, but if we're not truly walking with Him, our perspective starts to get off-kilter. When our thinking starts to get off, it's easy to become frustrated with our life and ungrateful for our circumstances! I can understand why the lost people around us have no joy – they have no hope! Yes, this world seems like it's gone crazy, but as Christians, we know that our life here will pass, and we'll spend an eternity in heaven!

In Psalms 16:11 we read that in God's presence is fulness of joy. Galatians 5:22 tells us that joy is a fruit of the Spirit; it's a byproduct of being filled with the Spirit. When we are truly walking with God and submitted to His Spirit, we'll have an abundance of joy that only He can give, even in tribulation (2 Cor. 8:2)! If we continually seek the Lord and His strength (Ps. 105:4), His joy will be our strength (Neh. 8:10). We should be a light to those around us; our joy should make people want what we have! It's important that we keep Christ first in our lives and daily enter His presence. As we continually walk with Him, we will have joy that only He brings!

joy

Date:

Scripture:

On My Heart:

Today's Application:

Prayers:

Blessings:

Unspeakable Joy – During Life's Deepest Trials

By Lydia L. Riley

---

*That the trial of your faith, being much more precious than of gold that
perisheth, though it be tried with fire, might be found unto praise and honour
and glory at the appearing of Jesus Christ: Whom having not seen,
ye love; in whom, though now ye see him not, yet believing,
ye rejoice with joy unspeakable and full of glory:*

I Peter 1:7-8

I ask you to travel back into time, turning the pages of the book
of your life. What is that darkest chapter, the page stained with the
most tears, perhaps the hidden deepest sorrow that only a few may
know about, or perhaps that sudden raw tragedy through which you
had to walk open for all the world to see? If you are a child of God,
we each will have our moment of fire – burning, ravishing, raging
fire – fire that destroys and brings great hurt and sorrow – yet this
is the same fire that God uses in our lives to refine and purify the
treasured vessel before Him.

Have you noticed that often the most joyful and most dedicated Christians are the ones who have walked through the deepest heartaches and most painful losses? Often, we only see the success and the glory of a seasoned saint of God – the glow of the gold. Yet, if they were to begin to share with you their testimony, turning back the pages of time - that deep trial of their faith, that "fiery trial" that forever changed their lives - comes to the surface of their story.

What is the key? How do you come through the fire rejoicing with joy unspeakable and full of glory? Why do some become bitter, angry, and aged beyond their years, while other Christians come forth with praises on their lips giving honor to their God for His faithfulness? How can we experience the glow and beauty of victory evidenced in everything we touch for the Lord? I believe the key is found in these verses – tucked right in between the two prevailing thoughts – two powerful words: "yet believing." This is the key! This is the path to prevailing victory through our tears! Yes, there is pain and hurt in the FIRE, but notice their FOCUS, on the One whom having not seen they love! Notice their FAITH in this One that they love – it is all about faith – remember, this is "the trial of your faith." Imagine that God Almighty counted you faithful to enter a little into His sufferings, to prove that your faith in Him and His Word would remain true and unshakeable! "Yet believing"– Do not let this deep trial shake your faith in Him – "ye rejoice with joy unspeakable..." This unspeakable joy – does that mean perhaps

YES.
THERE IS PAIN AND
HURT IN THE FIRE
BUT NOTICE THEIR
FOCUS ON
THE ONE WHOM
HAVING NOT SEEN
THEY LOVE!

it is so personal, so fulfilling, so exceedingly abundant, simply too much to try to express? Dear Christian, keep believing! God has not finished writing your story!

I Peter 4:12-13 "Beloved, think it not strange concerning the fiery trial which is to try you, as though some strange thing happened unto you: But rejoice, inasmuch as ye are partakers of Christ's sufferings; that, when his glory shall be revealed, ye may be glad also with exceeding joy."

joy

On My Heart:

Today's Application:

Prayers:

Blessings:

Joyful Remembrance

By Marissa Patton

Restore unto me the joy of thy salvation; And uphold me with thy free spirit.

Psalms 51:12

Remember the day you got saved? That peace that flooded your soul? The weight that was lifted off as the sin vanished away? The joy that filled your heart knowing that you had just been rescued from eternal damnation? I do. I remember it like it was yesterday. I remember that as a six-year-old little girl, I was ready to take on the world. I was smiling from ear to ear. And I stayed smiling for a long time. Why? Because I realized that I had just received the greatest gifts of all time - eternal life and a Father for a literal lifetime.

So why do we not go back and relive that day in our hearts more often? Why do we not take a step back from the daily grind? Take a step back in time to relive or "restore" that joy; the joy that only comes from being a child of the King. No

"JOY THAT ONLY COMES FROM BEING A CHILD OF THE KING."

matter the situation and no matter the struggle, I think as a Christian lady we should constantly be going back to the day of our salvation. Ask the Lord to revive your memory of all the sweet details of your changed life. Because that, my dear sister, is where we can find real, everlasting joy!

Take a moment and write down the emotions you felt as a new Christian.

joy

Date:

Scripture:

On My Heart:

Today's Application:

Prayers:

Blessings:

The Mortal Enemy Of Your Joy

By Candance Voyles

Let all bitterness, and wrath, and anger, and clamour, and evil speaking, be put away from you, with all malice: And be ye kind one to another, tenderhearted forgiving on another, even as God for Christ's sake hath forgiven you.

Ephesians 4:31-32

"Now the God of hope fill you with all joy and peace in believing, that ye may abound in hope, through the power of the Holy Ghost." Romans 15:13

My husband and I were driving one day. We began to talk about joy. Joy is a common word in the vocabulary of a Christian. We experience joy in salvation and in our relationship with God. My husband summed up our conversation with this: "Our joy will last as long as the source of our joy lasts."

"Wow," I thought, "What truth!"

If the source of our joy is everlasting and eternal, our joy can be everlasting and eternal. If the source is temporal, so is that joy. If things, people, our status in life, or our circumstances are the basis for our joy, it will not last. Emptiness will be its replacement. If our joy is truly in Christ, it will exist as long as He does.

I did discover that there are enemies, such as grief, fear, anger, and circumstances beyond our control that can steal or overshadow our joy. I also discovered from personal experience that joy can exist in the heart along with, and in spite of, these enemies. In grief, we have the Holy Spirit to comfort and soothe. We lean on that joy to sustain us. In fear, we trust the Unseen Hand to guide and protect. In anger, we are encouraged by the Word of God to "sin not" and not let the sun go down on our wrath. In our circumstances, we trust the process of being conformed to the image of the Savior. During each of these, we patiently allow the Lord to do His perfect work while joy coexists in our hearts.

But there is an enemy that joy cannot coexist with in the Christian heart. This enemy steals Joy completely away. The enemy is sin - more specifically, the sin of bitterness.

Bitterness is extreme enmity, a grudge, hatred, and painful affliction (Hebrews 12:15). It is a result of unforgiveness. It is a cancerous environment of the heart that will kill the joy until only hardness and emptiness remain. When that "root of bitterness" takes hold in our hearts, we see only what bitterness allows us to see-the worst in humanity. We forget that God knows all about every human. He chose to love us so much that He gave His only precious Son to redeem us. To maintain joy and resist bitterness, we must first have the mind of Christ - the Lamb of God who forgives so lovingly. We must dig out that root at its source. We must guard

IF THE
SOURCE OF
OUR JOY IS
EVERLASTING
AND ETERNAL,
OUR JOY CAN BE
EVERLASTING
AND ETERNAL.

against the thing that would cause it. Then we must allow the love of God to govern our hearts.

We have all been hurt at some point. We have all experienced some sort of betrayal that will fester and destroy our joy if we hang on to it. I have experienced the death of a precious loved one at the hands of another. So, dear friend, I know. I promise you. I know what it is to have to dig out that root and refuse to allow it to steal joy and control my heart. And it isn't always a one-time thing, but rather a continual guarding of the heart. Only a forgiving heart controlled by God's presence can truly have the power to love and forgive as Christ does.

How do we deal with bitterness? We shift our focus. We make a choice to look at Christ rather than the storm and the waves. That is the only way not to go under and sink into the abyss of bitterness. We pray fervently. We dig it out. Dig it out. Dig it out. No matter how many times it takes. We remind ourselves of the goodness of God how lovingly He forgives our sin and failures. We thank Him! And we forgive - as God for Christ's sake has forgiven us. Bitter waters and sweet waters cannot come from the same fountain.

John wrote in I John 1:4, "and these things write we unto you, that your joy may be full." Dear Sister, I encourage you to root out any bitterness you may have so that your joy may be full. Remember, joy can exist with many enemies. But joy cannot exist with bitterness.

joy

Date:

Scripture:

On My Heart:

Today's Application:

Prayers:

Blessings:

Be Strong, Girl!

By Deborah South

Then he said unto them, Go your way, eat the fat, and drink the sweet, and send portions unto them for whom nothing is prepared: for this day is holy unto our Lord: neither be ye sorry; for the joy of the LORD is your strength.

Nehemiah 8:10

Ezra and Nehemiah both wrote during a difficult time in the life of the children of Israel. They had returned from Babylonian captivity to find that their beloved city had been destroyed by their enemies. At this time, they had a choice to make: sit in anger and astonishment at what they had lost, or get busy doing what they could to restore things as much as possible. They began working! It wasn't easy, and it wasn't fun. I am sure they had many days of back-breaking labor, but anything worth having is worth working for. Through all of this time, Ezra and Nehemiah would write about the joy the people had. Some expressed their joy with shouting and some with weeping. There was joy in dedicating the house of the Lord and in feasting. (Ezra 3:12, 3:13, 6:16, 6:22). The joy of the Lord was their strength!

Nehemiah 12:43b, "...God made them rejoice with great joy: the wives also and the children rejoiced: so that the joy of Jerusalem was heard even afar off." The enemies even heard of the joy in

Jerusalem! There was something different about these people of God. They had a joy that the world does not understand.

They had plenty of reasons not to rejoice. There was trouble, heartache, disaster, and ashes. Yet, these people choose joy! Isn't it interesting that Nehemiah pointed out that the wives and the children rejoiced? I believe the rejoicing of the ladies made the work go smoothly, and the children joined in with the excitement that they saw in their mothers! (That is completely my opinion, of course.)

Today, you may be faced with troubles that you cannot see your way through. Choose joy. You may be caring for sick or disabled family or friends. You may be dealing with sickness in your own body. Perhaps there are financial distresses or problems in your church. Choose joy. No circumstance should change your joy. Jesus is the only true Source of joy. He gives full and lasting joy. He will give you the strength to choose joy!

I am not telling you to walk around with a fake smile plastered on your face. I am telling you to make a choice – choose joy! The world wants you to fall apart and be depressed. They want you to indict God as being unjust. They want you to choose misery and discouragement. They do not want you to rely on God's strength. You have a choice – choose joy!

Paul admonished us in Philippians 4:4, "Rejoice in the Lord alway: and again I say, rejoice." Paul was in prison, and yet he gives us a good command to obey: rejoice!

Strengthen yourself today with the reminder that "the joy of the Lord is your strength," and be strong, girl!

joy

Date: _____

Scripture: _____

On My Heart:

Today's Application:

Prayers:

Blessings:

Joy vs. Happiness

By Courtney Womack

These things have I spoken unto you, that my joy might remain in you,
and that your joy might be full.

John 15:11

Joy - a state of peace despite circumstances.

Happiness - a good feeling due to current circumstances.

True joy is often mistaken for happiness. Happiness is a good feeling that overcomes us when certain situations, circumstances, or events happen to be in our favor. Happiness quickly fades when those same events happen to not be in our favor. In contrast, joy is tranquility no matter what is happening to us, around us, or against us. Joy can include happiness but is not limited when happiness cannot be found. Joy can provide happiness, peace, comfort, and encouragement depending on what is needed at the time. Happiness relies on circumstances in life, while joy does not waiver with our circumstances.

Have you ever had a time in your life that you felt like you had no joy? Did it seem, no matter how hard you tried, you were constantly struggling with life? The different phases of life tend to cause continual struggles and we often find ourselves in different circumstances than we would wish (Psalm 5:11). Even during these struggles and problems, we can STILL keep our joy! It is during these moments of life, whether we are on the top of the mountain or going through a valley that we have to decide whether we are going to have true joy.

I think of joy like a well. We need water to be healthy and thrive. The well is what gives us the water. In life, there are days when we are naturally more thirsty. We have done more physical work, we have given more effort, and so often on those days we need more water. If we are out of water but need it, where would we go? That's right! To the well. We have to get our water from the well, we can't supply it ourselves. Due to the circumstances of life, we will have days that we need to dig down deeper for joy and on other days it is just flowing freely. Isaiah 12:3, says "Therefore with joy shall ye draw water out of the wells of salvation." When we have Jesus in our hearts we always have the ability to draw true joy from His well. Instead of trying to make every day "happy," let's choose to dig down in the Word and into our wonderful Saviour to get our true joy! His joy will last so much longer than just simple happiness.

"HAPPINESS RELIES ON CIRCUMSTANCES IN LIFE. WHILE JOY DOES NOT WAIVER WITH OUR CIRCUMSTANCES."

joy

Date: _____

Scripture: _____

On My Heart:

Today's Application:

Prayers:

Blessings:

Joy In Belief

By Kate Ledbetter

And my soul shall be joyful in the Lord: it shall rejoice in his salvation.

Psalm 35:9

I have heard it said that happiness is momentary, but joy is eternal. When I was thinking of this it brought a smile to my face. It also had me wondering, "What is the opposite of joy from a Biblical perspective?" I know that the opposite of happiness is sadness, but I had no clue what the opposite of joy was. So I did what most people in this day and age do; I simply looked up, "What is the Biblical antonym for joy?" The definition I found helped me to see Scripture I have read so many times in a new light.

The biblical opposite of joy is unbelief. When we choose to lay down our belief that God is in control of everything, we forfeit our joy. Joy is found in belief. This is why in so many of the Psalms, David could lay his heart before the Lord and seemingly be lost in the weight of his situation. Then, as if struck by the reality of Who he is speaking to, his tone changes. Instead of pouring out what

JOY
IS
FOUND
IN
BELIEF.

could easily lead to unbelief, he anchors himself in the joy of Who God is to him.

Read Psalm 35 and focus on this verse and the placement of verse 9:

"And my soul shall be joyful in the Lord: it shall rejoice in his salvation." Psalm 35:9

The question I found myself asking is how do I walk in joy? In the hard times, do I walk in fear and worry, full of unbelief? Or, do I choose joy ("to spin around" as the word "joyful" literally means)? Do I choose to remember that though the situation may seem hard, the enemies may be many and the friends few, and this flesh may be weary and weak, that in joy I can look to The One Who is ALWAYS in control? I can choose to simply believe that whatever is happening is all part of His Master plan. Then, with David I can say (in the midst of all the trouble), "And my soul shall be joyful in the LORD: it shall rejoice in his salvation." The joy comes in simply believing that God can and that God will.

Do you believe God can? What are you going through today that He cannot take care of in His time and in His way? Do not lay down your joy for unbelief. Rejoice now in His salvation. GOD CAN!!!

joy

Date:

Scripture:

On My Heart:

Today's Application:

Prayers:

Blessings:

Jesus, Others, and You

By Brittney Young

Looking unto Jesus the author and finisher of our faith; who for the joy that was set before him endured the cross, despising the shame, and is set down at the right hand of the throne of God.

Hebrews 12:2

The Lord himself gives us a perfect example!

J- Jesus

O- Others

Y- You

When I think of the word joy, I am reminded of the little acronym I learned as a child. Though simple it may seem, it is very important in our Christian walk.

However, if I am honest, it took me several years in my Christian walk to have a better understanding of the word joy. In fact, it can be easy to mistake the difference between joy and happiness.

I remember a specific year in my life when the struggle was real! I struggled with myself, with people, and with circumstances.

All I could see around me was the black cloud of negativity and I was just discouraged with life, and the burdens it can bring. While out shopping one day, the phrase hit me like a ton of bricks! It seemed to be on everything I was seeing in the store ...choose joy!

How do I choose joy? I pondered that thought! Conviction set in my heart! I realized I was not choosing joy, I was choosing to see all the negative things. I wasn't allowing the joy of the Lord to be my strength. I had become weak in my flesh.

Happiness is based on circumstances, but joy is what was placed in your heart the day the Lord saved you! I had it all wrong. I wasn't missing Joy, I was just not choosing it!

We know the Devil would desire nothing more than to steal your joy, but he can't! It is mine to keep, but I must remember to choose it and not push it away when unpleasant circumstances cloud my vision! Our happiness may come and go, but what the Lord did for me on April 9th, 2000 as an 11 year old girl, no one can steal!

In conclusion, I am reminded of the verse in Hebrews 12:2, "Looking unto Jesus the author and finisher of our faith; who for the joy that was set before him endured the cross, despising the shame, and is set down at the right hand of the throne of God."

The Lord himself gives us a perfect example! Who for the joy that was set before him endured! How did my Lord have joy in what he was enduring and suffering for you and me? He knew what was set before Him and knew the Joy that would come when God's perfect plan is fulfilled!

So when the going gets tough we need to remember the joy that is set before us! One day the hardship of this life will be over and we will have joy unspeakable, but until that day, endure for the Joy that is set before you and choose joy!

joy

Date:

Scripture:

On My Heart:

Today's Application:

Prayers:

Blessings:

About The Authors

Each author has been handpicked because of their testimony
for Christ. God has gifted each writer with incredibly versatile
perspectives of the Christian life. These godly ladies come from
all walks of life including pastor's wives and daughters,
missionary wives, church staff ladies, and faithful church
members. Their written words of wisdom are sure
to bless your heart.

To know more about our writers please visit:

thehighlyfavouredlife.com/our-story

Salvation Made Simple
By Renee Patton

Admit. One must first admit they are a sinner. Romans 3:10 states, "As it is written, There is none righteous, no, not one." Sin is everywhere and we all commit sin, many times without even trying. Perhaps in a conversation, we say something innocently, then realize it was not correct. That, my friend, is lying. Of course, murder is a sin that is seen and felt by those affected. However, lying is too. Jeremiah reminds one that "The heart is deceitful above all things, and desperately wicked: who can know it?" (17:9). A baby does not have to be told how to sin, it is simply in our nature. One must admit they are a sinner otherwise we make God a liar as found in I John 1:10, "If we say that we have not sinned, we make him a liar, and his word is not in us."

Believe. One must believe Jesus came to this earth to be born and die for our sins. "For God so loved the world, that he gave his only begotten Son, that whosoever believeth in him should not peish, but have everlasting life" (John 3:16). God desires that we should not perish, thus the choice is ours. God gives man the opportunity for salvation if man would take it. Romans 5:8 states "But God commendeth his love toward us, in that, while we were yet sinners, Christ died for us." Webster's 1828 Dictionary defines commendeth as entrusts or gives. So, God gave us His love through His Son, Jesus. Furthermore, Romans 5:19 shows how sin came from Adam and is made righteous through Christ, "For as by one man's disobedience [Adam] many were made sinners [mankind], so by the obedience of one [Jesus] shall many [mankind] be made righteous."

Confess. Confession is made with one's own mouth. The words must come from the person alone. Romans 10:9 talks of both confession and believing, "That if thou shalt confess with thy mouth the lord Jesus, and shalt believe in thine heart that God hath raised him from the dead, thou shalt be saved." The key is I have to confess to God. My husband or friend cannot confess for me. While God gives man the opportunity on earth, there will be a time every knee will bow and confess God is Lord, "For it is written, As I live, saith the Lord, every knee shall bow to me, and every tongue shall confess to God" (Romans 14:11).

To see more resources on salvation visit:
https://www.thehighlyfavouredlife.com/simple-salvation

If you made this decision, please contact us at *highlyfavouredlife @gmail.com.*
We would love to rejoice with you in the new life you now have in Christ.

www.ingramcontent.com/pod-product-compliance
Lightning Source LLC
Chambersburg PA
CBHW060323050426
42449CB00011B/2619